IMMIGRATION
IN AMERICA

ASYLUM, BORDERS, AND CONFLICTS

by Danielle Smith-Llera

Consultant:
Daniel Stageman, PhD,
John Jay College of Criminal Justice

COMPASS POINT BOOKS
a capstone imprint

Informed! is published by Compass Point Books, an imprint of Capstone.
1710 Roe Crest Drive
North Mankato, Minnesota 56003
www.capstonepub.com

Library of Congress Cataloging-in-Publication Data is available on the Library of
Congress website.
ISBN: 978-0-7565-6415-5 (library binding)
ISBN: 978-0-7565-6562-6
ISBN: 978-0-7565-6416-2

Summary: Immigration is a hot topic in the United States. What kind of immigration
should be allowed? How should immigrants who have come into the United States
illegally be treated? What about the Dreamers? Refugees seeking asylum? Will
building a border wall keep out undocumented immigrants and stop the flow of drugs
into the U.S.? Might improving technology offer a better answer? Students will learn
about the issues surrounding immigration and border security while discovering how
they can get involved in helping to find a solution.

Image Credits
Alamy: Historic Collection, 17, Marmaduke St. John, 31, Science History Images,
22; Getty Images: The Washington Post, 5; iStockphoto: Photo Beto, 10; Library
of Congress: 19, 21; Newscom: picture-alliance/dpa/Bruno Gallardo, 39, Picture
History, 18, Polaris/US Army/Tawanna Starks, 37 (bottom), Reuters/Adrees Latif,
33, Reuters/Jonathan Alcorn, 54, Reuters/Kevin Lamarque, 29, Sipa USA/Ronen
Tivony, 49, UPI/Ariana Drehsler, 45, ZUMA Press/Charles Reed, 26, ZUMA Press/
Erik Lesser, 25, ZUMA Press/Kris Grogan, 37 (top), ZUMA Press/Office Of Inspector
General, 41, ZUMA Press/Roberto Bonet Negrete, 9; North Wind Picture Archives:
15, 16; Shutterstock: Arthimedes, cover, Arthur Greenberg, 7, Dan Holm, 50,
Hernando Sorzano, 34, Mark Reinstein, 52, Rebekah Zemansky, 6, Sherry V Smith, 13,
ShotStalker, 44
Design Elements: Shutterstock

Editorial Credits
Editor: Michelle Bisson; Designer:Brann Garvey; Media Researcher: Eric Gohl;
Production Specialist: Kathy McColley

Consultant Credits
Daniel Stageman, PhD, John Jay College of Criminal Justice

All internet sites appearing in back matter were available and accurate when this book
was sent to press.

Printed and bound in the USA.
PA99

TABLE OF CONTENTS

Chapter One

Hatred in Plain Sight

Cactus plants rise out of the dry earth of the southern Arizona desert. Summer temperatures can reach 125 degrees Fahrenheit (52 degrees Celsius). Winter temperatures can drop below freezing at night. Customs and Border Protection (CBP) officers found 14-year-old Marco there alone in January 2019. They asked if he was thirsty, hungry, or afraid. The boy told them he had traveled by car and bus more than 2,000 miles (3,219 kilometers) from his home country of Guatemala. He hoped to live in Kentucky where his brother had settled. But he did not have permission to cross the border onto U.S. soil.

The southern border the U.S. shares with Mexico is 1,900 miles (3,058 km) long. The 4,000-mile (6,437 km) northern border with Canada is the longest barrier between countries in the world. Fences can mark these borders. Bodies of water such as the Rio Grande or the Great Lakes can too. Sometimes only a sign identifies the border. But

Marco (in black jacket) is one of many teenagers who have fled their troubled home countries. As have immigrants in times past, these teens hope to find a better life in the U.S.

often nothing marks the line between two nations in southern deserts and northern forests.

Dangerous terrain frightens people attempting to cross without documents. But customs officers can be frightening too. They wear bulletproof vests and carry weapons. They patrol the borders on horseback, jet skis, in off-road vehicles, helicopters, and planes. They follow people's tracks through snow, mud, and sand. They learn to speak Spanish to find out people's stories and how they arrived at the U.S. border.

FACT

Undocumented immigrants have been called *illegal immigrants* or simply *illegals*. The word *illegal* is often considered offensive, as the word can describe actions, but not human beings. Human beings are neither legal nor illegal.

People sometimes wait for hours to cross the border from Mexico into California.

Easy Crossing

The largest border crossing in the U.S. is located near San Diego, California. It is also one of the busiest in the world. Almost 95,000 people cross into the U.S. from Mexico at the San Ysidro port of entry every day. They travel by car—or by foot—along a wide pedestrian walkway built by the U.S. government. Everyone must show CBP officers important documents. They must prove they have permission to enter the U.S. by land, air, or sea. CBP officers admit more than 1 million visitors through about 300 ports of entry every day.

Crossing the border the U.S. shares with Mexico can be perilous. There are often border patrol agents waiting to arrest people without documentation.

Anyone crossing the border must have a passport. It is created in a person's home country. It includes a person's full name, age, gender, and place of birth. With this information, U.S. border officials can check computer records. Someone who has committed crimes may be barred from crossing into the U.S. Border officials also check these databases to see if travelers may be dangerous. They may be members of groups that sell illegal drugs or have committed acts of terrorism.

A passport also proves a person's citizenship. Citizens from almost 40 countries need only a passport to enter the U.S. But all others must visit offices managed by U.S. government officials in their home countries. Inside these U.S. embassies and consulates, they pay a fee and submit an application to visit, work, or study in the U.S. If the application is approved, they receive a visa. Visas give them permission to stay in the U.S. temporarily. But some people arrive at U.S. points of entry without these documents. CBP does not allow them to freely enter the country. CPB turned away close to 125,000 people from the southwest border during a year-long period ending in 2018.

However, most people living in the U.S. without permission entered with visas. They become undocumented immigrants as soon as they stay past the date printed on their visa. About two thirds of undocumented immigrants have overstayed their visas, experts estimate.

Risky Paths

Migrants without visas cannot cross official checkpoints. They find other ways to cross. The Rio Grande and the Colorado River form two thirds of the border between the U.S. and Mexico. Swiftly moving water can be more dangerous than any human-made barrier. Still, migrants attempt to cross in flimsy boats, without life preservers. In May 2019, a raft carrying nine people from Honduras flipped into the Rio Grande. An adult and three young children were swept away and drowned.

Unfortunately, this fate is common. In 2018, CBP officers responded to 4,300 emergencies along the southern border. They are not always able to rescue migrants from drowning, heat stroke, and dehydration. CBP reported that more than 7,500 migrants had died along the southwestern border from 2008 to 2018. Humanitarian groups estimate that number is actually much higher.

Crossing the northern border might seem less

People travel from their countries by various methods. This group of Central American immigrants attempted to cross the Rio Bravo from Mexico to get to the U.S. Border agents rescued them in the middle of the river.

challenging. Canadian government officials have granted visas to visitors more easily than U.S. government officials. Some migrants fly to Canada, then head south to the U.S. border. But Canada's thick forests, frigid lakes and rivers, and subfreezing temperatures can make this border deadly for migrants too. Still, the number of people apprehended along the U.S.-Canada border nearly doubled in one year from 2017 to 2018.

Migrants need help to cross dangerous and unfamiliar terrain. They often turn to human smugglers. For a fee, smugglers transport migrants illegally to destinations deep inside the U.S. But their help costs thousands of dollars per person. Human smugglers may treat their customers with carelessness. For example, smugglers ordered a 17-year-old girl to jump from the top of a border fence near Arizona. It was 30 feet (9 meters) high, and she broke her spine. Smugglers often demand that migrants pay additional money

Migrants are often smuggled across the border in trucks. Mexican customs officials sometimes use dogs to check vehicles that cross the border.

FACT

CBP officers inspect more than 67,000 cargo containers every day with the help of handheld X-ray scanners and drug-sniffing dogs. More than $3 trillion in legal goods pass across borders each year. Every day, CBP halts almost 6 tons of illegal drugs from entering the U.S. They have been found in unexpected places, such as inside a truck's spare tires and under a load of cucumbers.

on the way to the border. Migrants who can't pay have been abandoned to die in the desert. In 2003, a group of smugglers loaded migrants into a truck's windowless compartment. Cargo usually travels there. On the way to Houston, Texas, temperatures spiked and 19 people died from heat and lack of water and air. If apprehended, smugglers can receive long prison sentences for victims' suffering, injuries, and deaths.

Crossing Over

Some migrants manage to cross the border despite surveillance towers, buried motion sensors, and infrared cameras. Once on U.S. soil, they are undocumented immigrants. Most undocumented immigrants travel to major urban areas such as New York, Los Angeles, Houston, and Dallas–Fort Worth. There they reunite with family members already living in the U.S. Many find jobs and soon the U.S. feels like home. But living in the U.S. without permission can be frightening.

On Her Own

Maryori Urbina-Contreras rode taxis to school to avoid the dangerous gangs that roamed her hometown in Honduras. But she could not escape the violence. When she was robbed at gunpoint, she feared for her life and knew she had to escape. At age 13, she walked, rode buses, and even took a boat to the U.S. to find family members living there. In 2014, she was one of 68,000 children who crossed the border. She asked for asylum the next year and was refused, as were 78 percent of Honduran asylum seekers that year.

Urbina-Contreras gave TV interviews and visited lawmakers in Washington, D.C., to explain the dangers she and others faced in Central America. Finally, in 2018, a judge in Chicago found that Urbina-Contreras's story proved she was part of a group targeted by violence in her home country: young, poor women. Outside the courthouse Urbina-Contreras draped a U.S. flag around herself and said in Spanish, "This is the flag that protects me. This is my home now."

Undocumented immigrants may live far from CBP officers patrolling borders. But another law enforcement agency oversees immigration inside U.S. borders. Some officers in U.S. Immigration and Customs Enforcement (ICE) can send undocumented immigrants back to their home countries. ICE also forces migrants to wait in detention centers until a judge decides whether they should be deported. By law, they usually have a chance to explain to a judge why they should stay in the U.S.

Eyes on the Border

Even people who live far from U.S. borders care about immigration. Events at the borders grab headlines and spark fierce debate. They also help determine who wins elections. Some feel the government should restrict the flow of immigrants. They worry about border security and the 10 million or so undocumented immigrants living in the U.S. Others are concerned about the well-being of migrants who risk their lives to escape harsh conditions in their countries. They worry about how these immigrants are treated when they reach the U.S.

Immigration is not a new topic of debate. Immigrants have been joining the U.S. population for hundreds of years.

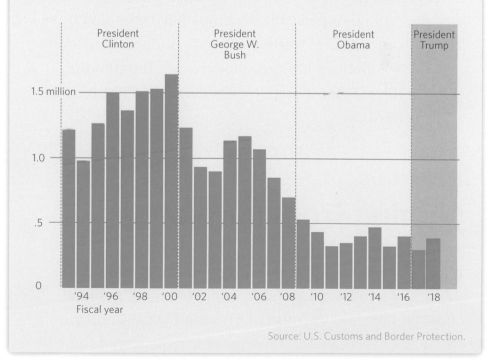

Despite physical barriers, thousands of migrants find ways to cross into the United States each year.

Total Number of Arrests for Illegally Crossing the Border Between the U.S. and Mexico

President Clinton

President George W. Bush

President Obama

President Trump

1.5 million

1.0

.5

0

'94   '96   '98   '00   '02   '04   '06   '08   '10   '12   '14   '16   '18

Fiscal year

Source: U.S. Customs and Border Protection.

Chapter Two

Hope and Struggle

About 14,000 years ago, the first people to arrive in North America may have walked from Asia to Alaska. Warmer weather and more plentiful food may have attracted them. They are ancestors of North America's indigenous peoples, including American Indians. Modern-day immigrants come to the U.S. for the same reasons: more opportunities and a better life.

Coming from Europe

Ships brought the first Europeans to North America in the early 1500s. Some left behind crowded, polluted cities for new opportunities. Others left because they were convicted of crimes and their governments forced them to leave. Many came for the freedom to practice their own religions. English and Dutch, Swedes, and other Europeans settled in the American colonies. As more immigrants arrived, these settlements became towns, then cities. European immigrants and their descendants later claimed most of the homelands where American Indians once lived.

Those who left the Netherlands and England in 1620 to travel to America are considered the first settlers. Really, however, they were the first immigrants to a land already inhabited by American Indians.

In 1790, the U.S. counted its population for the first time. The new nation also gathered information on the ethnicities of the population. About half of its 3.9 million residents were English immigrants or their descendants. The next largest group—almost 20 percent of the population—were Africans. Most of them were enslaved in the U.S. These African Americans or their ancestors had been kidnapped from their home countries. They were forced to come to the U.S. to work without pay and under brutal conditions. They helped to make the nation prosperous. Yet they were not allowed to become citizens. Two of the requirements for becoming a U.S. citizen were being free and white.

By the mid-1800s, steamships made the trip across the Atlantic Ocean faster and more affordable. More and more people were coming to the U.S. No federal immigration laws yet controlled the flow of immigrants. For Europeans, the U.S. offered escape from hardship. Revolutions in Europe in 1848 drove Germans to the U.S. Desperation brought more immigrants too. Their letters home also inspired more people to immigrate. By the 1860s, more than a third of all immigrants were Irish. Potato crops had failed in Ireland and starving people fled to the U.S.

In the mid-1800s, many Irish people came to the U.S. to escape starvation. At the time, many of those already in the U.S. denounced them as dirty criminals.

The nation depended on new immigrants to work difficult jobs on farms and in mines. In the late 1800s, new factories needed many hands to produce all the goods for a growing nation. These jobs demanded long hours in dangerous conditions. New immigrants from Italy, Poland, and other countries in those regions were eager for work. They often took these jobs. By 1920, half of all factory workers were immigrants or the children of immigrants.

But many longtime residents of the U.S. were alarmed by the newcomers. It made no difference that their own ancestors were immigrants. They resented that some practiced different religions, spoke different languages, or had darker skin. A political party based on anti-immigration beliefs formed in the mid-1800s. The American Party believed that immigrants should be deported if they broke laws or were poor. They said immigrants should not run for office. The government required immigrants to wait two years before applying for citizenship. But the American Party thought they should have to wait 21 years or more. Opponents called it the "Know Nothing Party." In the 1850s, voters elected party members to many state and local governments. Yet, they did not succeed in forcing the federal government to limit immigrants' freedoms.

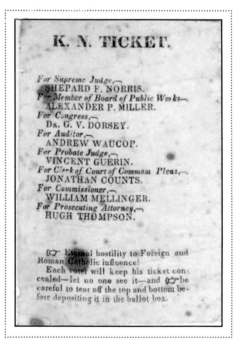

"Know Nothing Party" candidates ran on a platform that called for an end to "foreign and Roman Catholic influence."

Coming from the East

Chinese immigrants rushed to California when gold was discovered in the 1850s. They were eager to escape the food shortages and rebellions in their home country. They found jobs, including building railroads that stretched across the nation. In the 1860s Chinese immigrants continued to arrive to take jobs and open new businesses. But they faced racism from U.S.-born workers who were jealous of their success. Many U.S. residents also felt that the Chinese people's language, traditions, and religion were too different from their own. They believed these immigrants did not belong in the U.S.

Chinese laborers helped build the railroads that crisscross the U.S. and made the nation a great power. In return, they were not allowed to become citizens.

Anti-Asian discrimination triggered the first federal immigration laws. In 1882, Congress passed the Chinese Exclusion Act. It banned almost all Chinese immigration. It also banned Chinese residents from becoming citizens.

Meanwhile, immigration from other countries was on the rise. The government opened Ellis Island in 1892. Ships stopped at this immigration station in New York Harbor. More than 12 million immigrants would enter through this first official port of entry. But many U.S. residents were disturbed by the rising numbers of immigrants.

Descendants of the millions who entered Ellis Island as immigrants now talk about it proudly. At the time, those immigrants were greeted with hostility and fear.

In 1924, the federal government once more decided which immigrants were welcome—and which were not. Congress's Immigration Act of 1924 banned immigrants from almost all Asian countries. It also set strict quotas, limiting the number of immigrants allowed from various countries. This quota system gave the most visas to northern European immigrants. In other words, white, English speakers.

Coming from the South

The Immigration Act of 1924 did not limit the number of immigrants from Canada or other countries in Central and South America. But the law did create the first border patrol. Border stations were created to admit Mexican workers. They also collected visa fees and taxes from those entering. However, in its early years, the primary focus was on the Canadian border.

FACT

Armed groups other than the CBP have detained migrant families along the southwestern border. They are civilians who oppose undocumented immigrants and often embrace racism. In the 1800s, armed civilians patrolled the border to keep black people from escaping slavery and later to keep Chinese immigrants out of the U.S.

During World War II, the U.S. turned once again to new immigrants to fill necessary jobs. Thousands of Mexican immigrants joined the military as soldiers and pilots. They also took over farm work after many U.S. workers joined the military. Starting in 1942, the U.S. invited 4.6 million Mexican people through the "Bracero Program." They arrived to plant and harvest cotton, fruit, and vegetables on U.S. farms. The farm owners were pleased with the new situation. They could pay Mexican workers less than the salaries U.S. workers demanded. Meanwhile, these immigrants could earn 10 times what they could for the same work in Mexico. During the 20 years this program lasted, many Mexican temporary workers settled in the U.S. to live.

Mexican laborers were brought to the U.S. when it was convenient and deported when anti-immigrant sentiment rose after World War II.

After World War II, the government viewed people from foreign countries with suspicion. Even those already living and working in the U.S. faced discrimination. In 1954, the government deported approximately 1.1 million individuals. Many of them came from families that had lived for generations on U.S. land. Trains, buses, and planes transported them to Mexico.

Finding Refuge

The U.S. has often been a place of safety for refugees. Some of the earliest immigrants during colonial times were refugees. They left England because they were targets of hatred and violence because of their religion. Still, opening the borders to people fleeing danger in their home countries has sparked debate.

In the late 1930s, the U.S. quota system denied safety to refugees fleeing Nazi Germany's decision to murder millions of Jewish people. A ship carrying almost 1,000 Jewish people from Germany was turned away by the U.S. government in 1939. Some of its passengers returned to Europe, where hundreds died. Later in the war, the U.S. finally accepted hundreds of thousands of Eastern European refugees. In the mid-1950s, the U.S. allowed tens of thousands more immigrants, mostly from Western Europe. The McCarren-Walter Act of 1952 ended racial quotas. But the nation-of-origin quotas remained in the law. These quotas discriminated against most Catholics, Eastern Europeans, and Asians.

Congress took a dramatic step in 1965. It voted to end the quota system that favored white people over other races and ethnicities. President Lyndon Johnson signed the Immigration and Nationality Act in a ceremony at the Statue of Liberty. New immigrants approaching Ellis Island by ship always saw this landmark. Johnson said that the quota system "violated the basic principle of American democracy."

President Lyndon Johnson (left) ended the quota system that kept out most immigrants who were not white or from Western Europe.

The new law allowed 170,000 immigrants to enter the U.S. each year. Their home country no longer mattered. Over the next 50 years, the nation's diversity grew. In 1960, more than 80 percent of immigrants were born in Europe or Canada. By 2016, more than 85 percent of immigrants were from South and East Asia, Mexico, and other Latin American countries.

Becoming a Citizen

U.S. citizens cannot be deported. They can vote in elections and serve on juries. People are U.S. citizens if they are born in the U.S. or if their parents are U.S. citizens. Immigrants may apply to become citizens if they are at least 18 years old, have at least five years of legal U.S. residence, and have committed no serious crimes. Applying costs $725. A U.S. Citizenship and Immigration Services officer takes applicants' photographs, fingerprints, and digital signatures. Applicants must pass an interview and tests in English and civics. At a special ceremony, successful applicants pledge allegiance to the U.S. as new citizens.

This process is stressful for many immigrants. The application fee is high. They may not know English well. The information on the civics test may be new to them. And there is a further challenge. Under the Trump administration, the wait time for an interview has doubled to more than a year. About 9 million immigrants are eligible to apply, yet choose to remain in the U.S. as permanent residents. Instead of a U.S. passport, an ID called a "green card" allows them to cross U.S. borders freely.

Chapter Three

New Americans

More than 43 million immigrants live in the U.S., experts estimated in 2018. Of those, about 10.7 million are living in the nation without permission. This group of undocumented immigrants is the topic of intense debate: Do they harm or improve the nation's quality of life?

Money Matters

As in past centuries, U.S. business owners are eager for workers willing to do difficult jobs for low wages. The government tries to keep up. Each year, it grants 140,000 work visas for immigrants moving permanently to the U.S. The government also gives about 1.5 million visas to immigrants for temporary work each year. People who receive these visas work in many different roles, including agricultural workers, chefs, nurses, and engineers.

Many undocumented workers have been in the U.S. for decades. Their willingness to do seasonal work that most permanent residents won't do benefits both the workers and the farmers who hire them.

But undocumented immigrants are also able to find work. They can earn far more money in the U.S. than in their home countries. For example, earnings for factory workers in Mexico average about $2.50 per hour. Earnings for U.S. factory workers averaged more than $22.00 per hour in 2019. Workers can send money back to their home countries to buy property and help relatives. This money can transform immigrants' hometowns. For example, a home's concrete walls and sheet metal roofs can be replaced with brick and shingles. Almost $150 billion was sent by immigrants back to their home countries in 2017.

It takes only seconds for employers to check if job applicants have entered the country legally. The government runs an online database called E-Verify with that information. But using E-Verify is not required by all states for all employers. An estimated 7.8 million undocumented immigrants were working U.S. jobs in 2016. That's about 5 percent of the workforce. President Trump has a firm anti-immigration attitude. But as a businessman, he owns golf clubs that have employed undocumented workers. The president has denied knowing about them.

There are risks when employers hire undocumented immigrants. ICE can arrest and deport employees. Employers may also have to pay fines. But ICE workplace raids have not stopped employers from hiring more undocumented immigrants. Many can't find U.S. citizens to do the work. Crops have rotted in fields after undocumented farm workers were deported. Employers would rather pay a fine than lose their businesses.

In April 2019, ICE arrested 280 undocumented workers at the CVE Technology Group in Allen, Texas. It was one of the largest raids in more than a decade.

A Gentler Approach

In some small Central American towns, community leaders must work hard to convince teenagers to stay. "We know everyone wants to leave this place," says Marcos Ixtamer, director of a center for teens in Guatemala called the Stay Here Center. "That's why we're here." Thanks in part to hundreds of millions of dollars of U.S. aid money, they have taught students skills for jobs such as cutting hair and repairing computers. They have taught them to speak English for jobs in tourism. Aid money has also helped police combat gangs that draw young people to the drug trade.

However, U.S. leaders expected to see clear results: a drop in Central American migrants at U.S. borders. But it's unknown how successful the center has been so far. Without seeing clear results, the U.S. may cut off all aid. Young people will feel abandoned and desperate, causing migration to surge, say experts.

Many U.S. employers benefit from the work of undocumented immigrants. Often they are the only people willing to take certain jobs at the wages employers will pay. When there are lots of jobs available, many U.S. residents avoid the jobs that don't pay well. About 24 percent of housekeepers are undocumented. U.S. residents also avoid jobs that are dirty or dangerous. Undocumented workers make up more than half of the hired labor on farms and about 15 percent of construction workers. Since they take more dangerous jobs, they are injured at a higher rate than U.S.-born workers. Their fear of deportation can also lead to injury. They may not report unsafe workplaces to the government.

U.S. consumers benefit from the work of undocumented immigrants every day. One study found that thousands of dairy farms would close without undocumented workers. Milk prices might spike by 90 percent. Undocumented workers also help the economy by earning money and spending it. Businesses profit, and so does the government. Part of the cost of purchases such as gas or groceries goes to the government as sales tax. Job earnings are taxed too. Undocumented immigrants pay an estimated $11.6 billion a year in taxes.

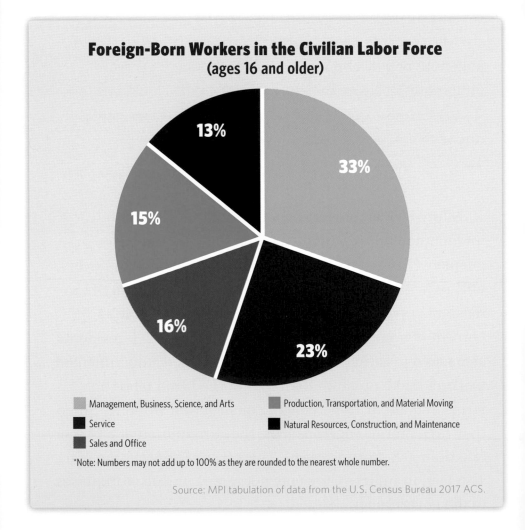

Foreign-Born Workers in the Civilian Labor Force
(ages 16 and older)

- Management, Business, Science, and Arts
- Service
- Sales and Office
- Production, Transportation, and Material Moving
- Natural Resources, Construction, and Maintenance

*Note: Numbers may not add up to 100% as they are rounded to the nearest whole number.

Source: MPI tabulation of data from the U.S. Census Bureau 2017 ACS.

What It Means to Be "American"

Despite their contributions to life in the U.S., immigrants face discrimination. They may be targets because of their race, ethnicity, or religion. They may also be targets if people suspect they are undocumented. They may hold beliefs about all undocumented immigrants that are unfair and untrue. Some U.S. leaders have encouraged these stereotypes.

The vast majority of immigrants are law-abiding citizens. Many, like Vietnamese immigrant Thu Tran of Falls Church, Virginia, own businesses.

Some people in the U.S. believe that undocumented immigrants are more likely to commit crimes. They have already broken a major law to enter the country, these people argue. Crossing borders without the permission of an immigration officer is a misdemeanor, or a minor crime. It is considered a major crime, or a felony, only when an undocumented immigrant reenters the country after having been deported.

FACT

All babies born inside U.S. borders are automatically U.S. citizens even if their parents are undocumented immigrants or on temporary visas. This right is protected by the 14th Amendment to the Constitution.

Chapter Four

Close the Borders?

A group of 7,000 exhausted Central American migrants neared the U.S. border in Tijuana, Mexico. It was November 2018. Over the past month they had walked and hitched rides for more than 2,000 miles (3,219 km) from Honduras, El Salvador, and Guatemala. Families, with an estimated 2,300 children, were part of the group. The trip was hard on everyone. Finding food and shelter was difficult. They risked being kidnapped by drug dealers or other criminals if they fell behind. But to the migrants, the journey was worth the risks. Poverty and gang violence were also a part of life in their home countries.

FACT

In 2019, CBP reported the number of migrants apprehended at the border from countries other than Mexico rose by 500 percent. These migrants were from 37 different countries, including India and the Democratic Republic of Congo. Waiting in Mexico to apply for asylum can be a challenge for migrants who do not speak Spanish.

Hundreds of Central American migrants traveled from Guatemala through Mexico to the United States despite efforts of the Mexican and U.S. governments to stop them. The migrants were fleeing terrible conditions in their countries.

President Donald Trump sent 5,800 U.S. soldiers to the southern border that November. He warned that "an invasion" was on its way. For Trump, the migrant caravan illustrated his view that immigrants were over-running the nation. His supporters, mostly Republican Party members, agreed with him. He said bluntly in 2019: "Our country is full." However, experts have found that the U.S. has room for more residents. The nation's U.S.-born residents are having fewer children. The U.S. population of undocumented immigrants has also declined. Between 1990 and 2007, 12.2 million undocumented immigrants lived in the U.S. By 2017, that population had dropped to about 10.7 million.

A Wall

Crowds have chanted "Build the Wall!" during Trump's speeches. He promised that, if elected, he would build a physical barrier between the U.S. and Mexico. Some of it was already there. Sections of walls and fences along the border date back to 1994. The oldest sections are made of recycled sheets of metal, chain link, and barbed wire. By 2010, the government had built an additional 600 miles (966 km) of border wall. By early 2019, 654 miles (1,052 km) had been built but many gaps remained.

Donald Trump campaigned on a promise to build a continuous wall between the U.S. and Mexico. It was a rallying cry at events even after he became president. Most of the wall remained unbuilt as his campaign for reelection began.

But most U.S. residents do not believe the border wall should be expanded. It would have no effect on the majority of the undocumented immigrant population. About twice as many undocumented immigrants overstay their visas as cross the southern border. Their home countries include Brazil, China, and India, among many others.

Opponents of a border wall also believe it's too expensive to build. Each mile of new steel wall costs more than $24 million. The border's steep river banks and mountains could prevent building stable structures there.

Opponents also argue that migrants are often desperate to cross barriers. They may not give up easily. Barriers do make it easier for border patrol officers to apprehend undocumented immigrants at busy border crossings in cities like El Paso. But in remote areas, people have climbed over barriers with ropes. They have also dug tunnels and cut openings with blowtorches to get past them. In 2018, 11 percent of people apprehended at the border tried again to enter the U.S.

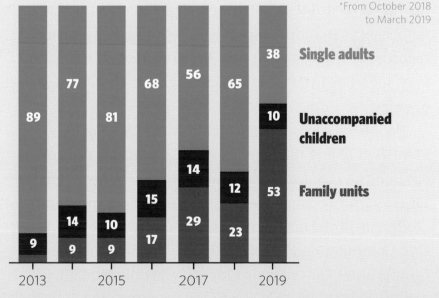

Most Arrests at the Southwest Border in the First Half of Fiscal 2019 Were of Families

% of apprehensions at southwest border through the first six months of fiscal year*, by type

*From October 2018 to March 2019

Single adults

Unaccompanied children

Family units

Source: U.S. Customs and Border Protection.

More than Walls

The terrorist attacks on September 11, 2001, forced the federal government to review border security. In the first days after, the U.S. government nearly closed the country's borders. Border officers inspected people's documents, belongings, and vehicles closely. People waited for hours in lines at the southern border. Some waited more than a day.

It is not practical to do such close inspections all the time. The U.S. economy depends on goods and people flowing smoothly across the border. Every day $1.4 billion worth of goods pass across 330 official ports of entry between the U.S. and Mexico. As many as 15 million U.S. jobs depend on trade with Mexico and Canada alone.

CBP officers must identify people who pose a high threat to the U.S. Scanners at land ports of entry also collect data from license plates. Booths at airports take photographs of passengers arriving on international flights. Scanners record their passports and fingerprints. Computer databases match this information with law enforcement records. Technology can save border agents' time. They may spend as little as 30 seconds with each person at ports of entry.

People who pose a high risk to the U.S. may be identified *before* they arrive. After all, the 9/11 terrorists entered the U.S. legally with student, tourist, and business visas. Airline companies must share the passport and credit card information of passengers flying to the U.S. Computer databases can identify undocumented immigrants. They can also identify people who have committed serious crimes or may be connected to terrorist groups. Some people worry that the government should not

Technology allows more effective surveillance. Here, U.S. border patrol agents are using the camera on a search helicopter to spot Central American migrants who crossed the Rio Grande illegally.

track so much personal information. Others believe giving up privacy is necessary for tough border security.

After 9/11, Presidents George W. Bush and Barack Obama spent billions of dollars to add more officers and technology along borders. Infrared cameras detect body heat. Ground sensors detect footsteps miles away from CBP stations. Satellites, blimps, and drones track movement from high overhead. But technology can never fully replace CBP officers. A CBP agent in Washington State prevented a would-be terrorist's plan to bomb the Los Angeles airport in 1999. The officer noticed a person behaving suspiciously as he drove off a ferry from Canada. Inspection of his car revealed explosives stored in the trunk.

Mobile surveillance cameras were deployed across the southern border of the U.S. to help spot—and stop—migrants crossing the border illegally.

Chapter Five

Open the Borders?

Migrants who arrive at U.S. borders do not always hide from CBP patrols. Instead, they search for them along the southern border and even at U.S. airports. These undocumented immigrants ask for a chance to enter the country legally. But how can they do so without a visa?

The Right to Asylum

Many people around the world face danger in their daily lives. This fear may drive them to look for another place to live. More than 25 million people worldwide could be on the move at any time as they search for protection in another country. U.S. law states that anyone on U.S.

soil has the right to request asylum if they fear returning to their home country. On this path, they avoid smugglers and dangerous terrain. They also have a chance to live and work in the U.S. legally.

So many asylum seekers were trying to enter the U.S. in 2018 that more than 6,000 of them had to wait for months, living in tents in Tijuana, Mexico, before they could be processed by U.S. customs agents.

Migrants in CBP custody must wait to see an immigration judge. They may be released to go freely into the U.S. until their court date. Or CBP officers may turn them over to ICE, whose officers place them in prison-like detention centers.

Once in court, undocumented immigrants must convince an immigration judge they deserve asylum. A wish to escape poverty does not qualify anyone for asylum. Asylum seekers must prove that they are in danger based on five categories: race, religion, nationality, political views, or membership in a particular social group, such as the LBGTQIA community. If the judge does not believe the threat against them is real, they are deported. If the judge believes them, they can stay. About 30 percent of applicants are allowed to stay to live and work in the U.S. They may apply to become permanent residents in one year.

Asylum seekers arriving at the southern border in early 2019 found lines of more than 1,000 people. The government had set up tent cities to house new arrivals. They would have had to wait days, even weeks or a month, to speak with CBP officers. And every day, thousands more migrants arrived.

Young Asylum Seekers

For decades, mostly undocumented young men arrived at the southern border. Decisions to deport could be made quickly. But asylum laws give special attention to children and their families while their applications are reviewed. The number of migrant children arriving at the border began to rise in 2014. In mid-2019, families with children made up 65 percent of apprehended migrants. Border officials struggled to house, feed, and care for them properly.

The nation watched, appalled, when a photo of the massive overcrowding of migrant families at a detention center in McAllen, Texas, was released in July 2019. Children were seen to have nowhere to lie down to sleep, or to clean themselves.

Children can arrive exhausted, dehydrated, ill, and anxious after difficult journeys to the border. There they have faced new hardships. Detention centers were designed decades ago to hold adults for short stays. They were not equipped to care for tens of thousands of children. They have had to sleep crowded onto mats on concrete floors under bright lights. They have had to wait in filthy conditions without soap, toothpaste, or toothbrushes. The Trump administration decided that these things were not necessities. Doctors have visited these centers. They say that such unhealthy environments are unsafe for children. By May 2019, seven children had died while in ICE detention. That happened in one year, after a decade in which no child had died in ICE detention.

Border officials and government leaders faced an enormous problem. More than 50,000 people were waiting in U.S. detention centers as of March 2019. Hundreds of thousands of cases waited for review in immigration courts. It would take years to get to them all. But people cannot wait that long imprisoned in detention centers. Under the U.S. Constitution, everyone in the nation has the right to fair treatment by the judicial system.

Too Young for a Big Job

Who cares for migrant children in detention centers without their parents? They must often take care of each other. That is what lawyers observed on a June 2019 visit to Texas detention centers. They interviewed 60 children. They hoped their stories would bring health inspectors to the detention facilities. They also hoped to bring more attention to the suffering that migrant children face in the U.S.

"A Border Patrol agent came in our room with a 2-year-old boy and asked us, 'Who wants to take care of this little boy?'" a detained teenage girl reported. Children as young as 8 years old were feeding, bathing, and changing the diapers of younger children. When a 5-year-old separated from her parents was weeping, a 15-year-old girl stepped in to help. "The workers did nothing to try to comfort her. I tried to comfort her and she has been with me ever since. [She] sleeps on a mat with me on the concrete floor. We spend all day every day in that room. There are no activities, only crying." A border officer laughed at children who cried, reported a 17-year-old boy.

Experts say the children who parent younger children face great stress. They are not mature enough for these responsibilities. What's more, they miss their parents too. One 14-year-old girl from Guatemala who had been holding two little girls in her lap told a reporter, "I need comfort too. I am bigger than they are, but I am a child too."

Different Attitudes

Supporters of asylum seekers believe the U.S. has a duty. It must not return people to countries where they face harm or death. Migrants from Honduras, El Salvador, and Guatemala leave countries that have some of the highest murder rates in the world. Gangs rule communities through fear and violence. Police often fear gangs too. Government officials offer little protection. They have even killed their own citizens who protest against them.

Immigration activists worry that many asylum seekers are treated unfairly by the U.S. About 75 percent of asylum seekers from El Salvador, Honduras, and Guatemala were denied in 2017. Meanwhile, only about 20 percent of Chinese asylum seekers were denied. Speaking English and hiring a lawyer gives some asylum seekers a better chance of receiving asylum.

Migrants take advantage of the asylum process, say Trump, his administration, and its mostly Republican supporters. Human smugglers promise migrant families that arriving with children protects them from deportation. Smugglers can pack buses with Central American migrants. Each migrant pays thousands of dollars for a safe and quick ride north. The driver leaves them within walking distance of the U.S. border, where they immediately request asylum. Some groups of unrelated adults and children present fake birth certificates. Smugglers provide them so they appear as a family. And by U.S. law, families cannot be held in detention centers for longer than 20 days. This is not nearly enough time for an immigration judge to decide if they can stay. So they will be released to wait in the U.S.

In the summer of 2019, the Trump administration issued a ruling that would reject asylum bids from refugees, such as those from Guatemala, who passed through another country on their way to the U.S. The rule was challenged, but a Supreme Court ruling in September 2019 allowed it to proceed temporarily.

President Trump has tried to make seeking asylum less inviting. He wanted to prevent adult asylum seekers from being released into the U.S. after 20 days. So, in 2018, he ordered ICE to separate children from their parents apprehended at the border. What was the reason? They had committed a misdemeanor: arriving at the border without proper documents. The federal government reported that 2,737 children were separated since it began counting in 2018. But that number is probably thousands higher. Without their children, parents could be held in adults-only detention centers for longer. The Trump administration hoped this cruel plan would discourage other undocumented migrant families from traveling to the border.

The journey to the United States is emotionally and physically challenging. These migrants had to hike up hills after making the first part of the journey from Guatemala in an inflatable raft.

Many in the U.S. and the world reacted with outrage to this inhumane treatment of migrants. Frightened children were transported to shelters or foster homes thousands of miles away from their parents. Images of crying children held in chain-link pens showed the world what was happening at the U.S. border. A federal judge ordered the child separation practice to end in June 2018. Yet migrant children continued to be separated from their parents.

Trump's harsh anti-immigration policies and threats have not solved challenges on U.S. borders. In fact, they may have made them worse. Many immigrants fearing new, harsher anti-immigrant policies may rush to the U.S. border in greater numbers.

A Stressed Border

The CBP directs many asylum seekers at the U.S. border to walk back into Mexico. There they add their name to a long waiting list. The Trump administration imposed strict limits on the number of migrants allowed into the U.S. each day to apply for asylum. But this did not speed up the process of reviewing applications. The result is thousands of migrants waiting at the border. They are homeless and struggle to keep hope. In May 2019, an estimated 13,000 asylum seekers waited in Mexico across from the U.S. border. By June, an estimated 19,000 were waiting. Adults and children slept in tents. They hoped CBP would call their names soon to start the asylum process. Their wait time could be months, even years.

Trump has discussed many other ways to discourage asylum seekers from approaching the border. He has said they should pay a fee for reviewing their asylum application. He has raised the idea of denying them permission to work in the U.S. while they wait for a decision. Many migrants waiting at the border grow desperate. They give up waiting for their turn and try to enter the U.S. illegally.

Most asylum seekers at the U.S. border in recent years are Central American. So Trump threatened to punish those countries. In March 2019, he announced a plan to cut about $500 million of aid to Honduras, El Salvador, and Guatemala. This money has helped improve the quality of life for citizens of those countries. It has funded schools, job training for teenagers, and health clinics. It has helped organize fair government elections and train police officers to combat crime. The money has helped build more roads and bring electricity to more communities. It has helped farmers face the effects of climate change. Rising temperatures and droughts have damaged crops. People facing hunger and poverty are more likely to move away.

Yet any decision Trump makes on immigration must survive the judicial system. As of May 2019, federal courts had blocked at least 25 actions Trump had taken on immigration. Some judges had even scolded the president for ignoring U.S. laws and the Constitution in handling asylum seekers.

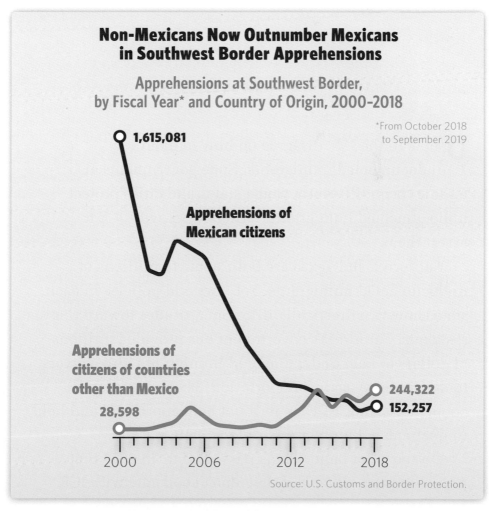

Non-Mexicans Now Outnumber Mexicans in Southwest Border Apprehensions

Apprehensions at Southwest Border, by Fiscal Year* and Country of Origin, 2000–2018

*From October 2018 to September 2019

1,615,081

Apprehensions of Mexican citizens

Apprehensions of citizens of countries other than Mexico

28,598

244,322

152,257

2000   2006   2012   2018

Source: U.S. Customs and Border Protection.

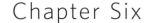

Chapter Six

Confusion at the Border

People in the U.S. disagree on how to handle undocumented immigrants. State governments also handle them differently. Some states and cities protect undocumented immigrants. Others work with ICE to arrest them.

California and Texas are both home to millions of undocumented immigrants. Yet laws and policies in each state show two drastically different attitudes toward these residents. California's government has provided millions of dollars to help undocumented immigrants hire lawyers to defend them against deportation. They also refuse to cooperate with ICE. They will not help apprehend and hold undocumented immigrants in local jails.

On the other hand, Texas passed a law in 2017 that punishes local officials if they don't cooperate with ICE.

They may pay high fines and even lose their jobs. Within other states, such as Florida, communities disagree over whether to protect undocumented immigrants from ICE or report them. "If you're an undocumented immigrant [in Florida], your life is now hugely dependent on where you live," said Muzaffar Chishti, the director of the New York office of the Migration Policy Institute. "It can come down to a few miles." This clash of opinions also takes place across the nation.

In California, protesters rallied in support of sanctuary for undocumented immigrants.

Another Wall

Some people favor strict limits on immigration, both legal and illegal. Several different kinds of immigrants have faced new challenges since President Trump took office. He has tried to block Muslim immigrants from entering the U.S., for example. He has also tried to limit the number of refugees fleeing war or natural disasters who are allowed into the U.S. Trump has also threatened to end a program that encourages immigration from countries not well represented in the U.S. population. In many ways, the Trump administration's new limits on immigration are similar to the quotas in place before the 1965 Nationality Act.

President Trump was elected in large part on his anti-immigration rhetoric. Many in the U.S. are strongly against allowing anyone to cross U.S. borders.

Trump's immigration policies have created an invisible wall, immigration activists say. It is not made of barbed wire and steel. It is created by rules and restrictions that block entrance to the U.S. more effectively than a physical border wall. For example, Trump has limited the number of visas issued for temporary work. Low-skilled workers determined to work in the U.S. may have to arrive without permission. Trump's new controls on immigration may have caused illegal immigration to surge. In March 2019, the number of undocumented immigrants apprehended at the border rose sharply to the highest level in 12 years.

But immigration activists believe there is a more practical and humane way to reduce illegal immigration. The government could make it easier for immigrants to receive visas. But Trump's administration has

made the process more difficult for applicants. Each year about 15 million people apply for visas to come to the U.S. About 65,000 of these applicants are considered high risk. They must submit detailed biographical information. They must also list social media usernames. As of 2019, all new applicants must give this information. Millions of people wait in their home countries for the U.S. government to review their visa applications. The wait time was three months in 2014. By 2019, it had increased to more than a year. These delays seem deliberate, some immigration lawyers say. They discourage new immigration.

This new process, or "invisible wall," hurts U.S. businesses. Employers might begin to hire workers outside the U.S. to do jobs at low wages. In mid-2019, the government suddenly announced an increase in visas for temporary workers. This statement left many confused. The president had just said that the U.S. had no room for immigrants. "On one hand, we need more people because the economy is booming," said immigration expert Alex Nowrasteh. "Then on the other hand, to say, 'The country is full, go back'—it's impossible to reconcile those."

Deciding Who Should Stay

No one without proper documents should be in the U.S., some Americans believe. They have broken the law by entering the country, even if the crime is only a misdemeanor. But capturing and deporting all undocumented people would carry a huge price. The cost of ICE apprehending, detaining, and transporting just one person is about $12,500. ICE officers deported more than 265,000 people in 2018. Deporting millions of people would cost billions of dollars.

More importantly, many people believe that removing most undocumented immigrants is unfair. These workers have contributed to the economy and diversity in the U.S., as immigrants have for hundreds of years. What's more, the U.S. has been their home for a long time. About 75 percent of undocumented immigrants have lived in the U.S. for more than 10 years. And that number is rising. Some Americans say the government should forgive them for entering without documentation. Many presidents and Congress members have agreed. In 1986, Republican President Ronald Reagan gave amnesty to almost three million undocumented immigrants. They had already lived in the U.S. for years. Legal permission to live in the

Though people now think of the Republican Party as being against undocumented immigrants, President Ronald Reagan, the "grand old man" of the party, gave amnesty to millions of undocumented immigrants.

U.S. gave these residents the chance to eventually apply for citizenship.

About one million immigrants find themselves in a difficult position. They have "Temporary Protected Status" and live in the U.S. However, they are not allowed to apply for citizenship. Some have fled war or natural disasters such as earthquakes. Another group of 800,000 immigrants also came to the U.S. for reasons outside their control. They came as children. Their parents are undocumented immigrants. They were also undocumented until 2012. That year, Democratic President Barack Obama introduced the Deferred Action for Childhood Arrivals (DACA) program. DACA protected these children from deportation. It also allowed them to go to school and to work in the U.S. They have served in the military. They have earned advanced degrees and often earn higher salaries than many U.S.-born workers. They pay a combined total of about $2 billion in taxes each year. These "Dreamers," as they are nicknamed, carry out their parents' dreams of a better life in the U.S.

When Trump called for the end of DACA in 2017, some political leaders were pleased. They believed the program rewarded the breaking of immigration laws. But others believed that Dreamers had grown up in the

FACT

Undocumented immigrants living in the U.S. do not often risk crossing the U.S. border again to visit their home countries. DACA program members Alvaro Morales and Frisly Soberanis travel to film their hometowns and loved ones. With these videos, they create a 360-degree virtual reality experience for participants in the Family Reunions Project.

Following the Dream

President Trump threatened to end the DACA program in 2017. On March 5, immigrants and their supporters held protests in Washington, D.C., and across the nation. One group of 11 DACA members—representing the approximately 11 million undocumented immigrants living in the U.S.—had walked more than 250 miles (402 km) from New York to join the protest. To many participants, the hundreds of people gathered felt like a celebration. "When you are an immigrant you feel so alone, and it feels amazing to see people from so many communities support us," said 18-year-old Nancy Canales, whose siblings are undocumented.

Some protesters wore white wigs and walked with canes to playfully symbolize their years of waiting to become permanent U.S. residents. Some members of Congress, mostly Democratic lawmakers, want border wall funding to be approved only if it includes a path for DACA members to become citizens. Amnesty and border walls cause such debate that bills to help DACA members continue to fail in Congress. But the Dreamers and their supporters won't give up. "We belong in this country," said DACA recipient Javier Gamboa. "It is a fight for my future."

U.S. and it was their true home. Federal judges ruled that Trump could not legally end DACA. They also called his plan cruel and wasteful. Members of Congress debated whether to pass a new law allowing Dreamers and others with Temporary Protected Status to apply for citizenship. But they could not agree. Instead, a case involving Dreamers was sent to the Supreme Court to decide.

A Divided Nation

How will the federal government treat undocumented immigrants living, working, and raising families in the U.S.? What will it do about the human suffering at the borders? These questions divide people across the U.S. Almost one quarter believe that immigration is the greatest challenge facing the nation, a 2019 poll found. The issue motivated Trump to allow a large part of the federal government to shut down for more than a month, ending in early 2019. In Congress, fierce disagreement on immigration—mostly between Republicans and Democrats—has prevented the passage of new immigration laws. As elected officials, members of Congress pay close attention to voters' opinions. They know that Donald Trump's anti-immigration views helped him get elected as president in 2016.

The majority of U.S. voters seem to want a balanced solution: laws that include both amnesty and border security. According to polls in 2019, three quarters of people believed in strengthening border security with more CBP officers. However, even more people—more than 80 percent—favored amnesty and a path toward citizenship for undocumented immigrants living in the U.S. They have voiced their opinions in protests across the country, including in the nation's capital. The slogan on their signs expresses a hopeful message: "Immigrants Are Welcome Here." But decisions on border security have remained anything but clear or unanimous.

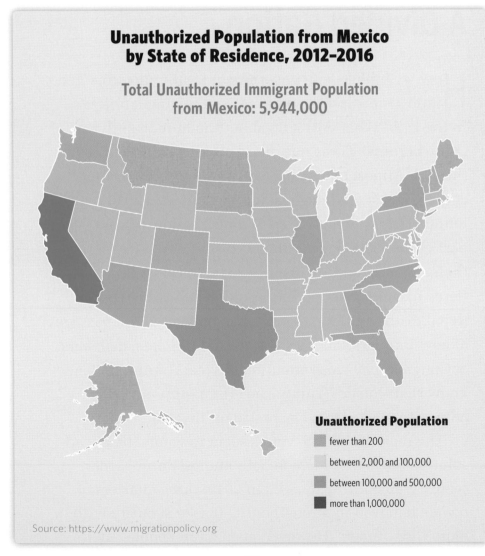

Unauthorized Population from Mexico by State of Residence, 2012–2016

Total Unauthorized Immigrant Population from Mexico: 5,944,000

Unauthorized Population

- fewer than 200
- between 2,000 and 100,000
- between 100,000 and 500,000
- more than 1,000,000

Source: https://www.migrationpolicy.org

GET INVOLVED

- Ask family members about your own immigration story. How did your ancestors come to the U.S.? Ask questions about other people's immigration stories too.

- Write your members of Congress a letter. Tell them your ideas about border security and immigration. For example, do you support expanding the border wall? Do you support or oppose DACA? Do you believe in amnesty for undocumented workers or are you against it?

- Join a local protest about immigration. You can make a poster with a phrase that expresses your opinions.

- Urge adults to consider their candidates' views on immigration before they vote.

- No matter what you believe about immigration and border security, stand up to racism and discrimination. Support classmates who may be targets due to their country of origin.

- Listen to the language people use to talk about people from other cultures. Speak up if it does not seem respectful of other cultures and diversity.

- Organize a school fundraiser to help children in detainment centers. The money you raise can help buy basic supplies such as toothpaste, clothing, and diapers.

- Keep up with news on immigration and border security. New information will help you develop your opinions about the topic.

GLOSSARY

amnesty—a pardon to a group of people

apprehend—to seize or arrest

asylum—a place of retreat and safety from danger

detain—to hold or keep someone, as in prison

deport—to legally remove someone from a country

enforce—to make a law effective

fiscal year—the period used by governments for accounting purposes; in the U.S. it's October to September

immigrant—a person who comes to live in a country where he or she was not born

migrant—a traveler from one area to another who is often looking for temporary work

passport—a document issued by a government that proves someone's identity and citizenship

smuggling—moving something or someone secretly and illegally

visa—permission given by a country to enter that country

Critical Thinking Questions

One group of U.S. residents opposes expanding the border wall, including some who support greater border security. Another group of people supports expanding the border wall. What factors could explain why these two groups have such different opinions about border security?

Living as an undocumented immigrant is known to cause stress. Besides the fear of deportation, many other parts of daily life are affected. In what ways can receiving citizenship help relieve that stress?

Many undocumented immigrants have lived in the U.S. Many such immigrants share American values and feel that the U.S. is home. What do you think being or feeling "American" means?

ADDITIONAL RESOURCES

Further Reading

Clark, Tea Rozman, Rachel Lauren Mueller, and Bao Phi. *Green Card Youth Voices: Immigration Stories from a Minneapolis High School.* Minneapolis, MN: Wise Ink Creative Publishing, 2016.

Kravitz, Danny. *Journey to America: A Chronology of Immigration in the 1900s.* North Mankato, MN: Capstone Press, 2016.

Osborne, Linda Barrett. *This Land Is Our Land: A History of American Immigration.* New York: Abrams Books for Young Readers, 2016.

Thi Bui. *The Best We Could Do: An Illustrated Memoir.* New York: Abrams ComicArts, 2017.

Internet Sites

Animated Map Shows History of Immigration to the U.S.
https://youtu.be/Fe79i1mu-mc

Beautiful interactive map of border wall construction history
https://www.washingtonpost.com/graphics/2018/national/
us-mexico-border-flyover/?utm_term=.7c513b76fd60

Simple website explaining visas
https://www.kids-world-travel-guide.com/visa-facts.html

SOURCE NOTES

p. 11, "This is the flag…" Elvia Malagon, "Immigration Judge Grants Asylum to Honduran Teen-Activist Who Fled Gang Violence at 13," *Chicago Tribune*, March 1, 2018, https://www.chicagotribune.com/news/ct-met-contreras-immigration-hearing-20180227-story.html Accessed August 5, 2019.

p. 22, "violated the basic principle…" "LBJ on Immigration," LBJ Presidential Library, October 3, 1965, http://www.lbjlibrary.org/lyndon-baines-johnson/timeline/lbj-on-immigration Accessed August 5, 2019.

p. 27, "We know everyone wants…" Kevin Sieff, "The Stay Here Center: A U.S.-funded school gives young Guatemalans job skills to find success in their own country. Will it keep them from migrating north?" *The Washington Post*, April 19, 2019, https://www.washingtonpost.com/news/world/wp/2019/04/19/feature/this-school-aims-to-keep-young-guatemalans-from-migrating-they-dont-know-its-funded-by-the-u-s-government/?utm_term=.7dc9a5d00e3c Accessed August 5, 2019.

p. 33, "an invasion…" "Migrant caravan: What is it and why does it matter?" BBC News, November 26, 2018, https://www.bbc.com/news/world-latin-america-45951782 Accessed June 3, 2019.

p. 34, "Build the Wall!…" G. Cristina Mora, "Immigration and Trump-Era Politics," Global Dialogue, October 28, 2017, http://globaldialogue.isa-sociology.org/immigration-and-trump-era-politics/Accessed August 5, 2019.

p. 42, "A Border Patrol…" Nicole Goodkind, "8-Year-Old Migrants Being Forced to Care for Toddlers in Detention Camps," *Newsweek*, August 5, 2019, https://www.newsweek.com/migrant-children-detention-camps-donald-trump-1445313 Accessed August 5, 2019.

p. 42, "The workers did nothing…" Chantal Da Silva, "Migrant Children Share Heartbreaking Stories of What It's Like to be Locked in U.S. Detention Centers: 'There Are No Activities, Only Crying'," *Newsweek*, June 28, 2019, https://www.newsweek.com/migrant-children-share-heartbreaking-stories-u-s-detention-1446447 Accessed August 5, 2019.

p. 42, "I need comfort too…" Ashley Fetters, "Childen Cannot Parent Other Children," *The Atlantic*, June 24, 2019, https://www.theatlantic.com/family/archive/2019/06/immigrant-children-border-parentification/592393/Accessed August 5, 2019.

p. 49, "If you're an undocumented…." Adam Edelman, "Sancutary Cities: Three States, Three Very Different Approaches," NBC News, October 8, 2017, https://www.nbcnews.com/politics/immigration/sanctuary-cities-three-states-three-very-different-approaches-n808406 Accessed August 5, 2019.

p. 51, "Each wave of newcomers…" "Immigration Reform," Nancy Pelosi: Speaker of the House, https://www.speaker.gov/issue/immigration-reform Accessed August 5, 2019.

p. 51, "invisible wall…" "Buy American and Hire American: Putting American Workers First," U.S. Citizenship and Immigration Services, https://www.uscis.gov/legal-resources/buy-american-hire-american-putting-american-workers-first Accessed August 5, 2019.

p. 51, "On one hand, we…" Mihir Zaveri and Emily S. Rueb, "U.S. Wants to Allow More Foreign Workers While Also Restricting Immigration," *The New York Times*, April 9, 2019, https://www.nytimes.com/2019/04/08/us/politics/trump-administration-h2b-visa.html Accessed August 5, 2019.

p. 54, "When you are an…" Alan Gomex and Sophie Kaplan, "DACA was supposed the end Monday. It didn't, but DREAMERs remain anxious," *USA Today*, March 5, 2018, https://www.usatoday.com/story/news/nation/2018/03/05/dreamers-daca-program-march-5-end/393280002/ Accessed August 5, 2019.

p. 54, "We belong in this…" Nicole Acevedo, "With no permanent immigration fix by DACA deadline, Dreamers amp political mobilization," NBC News, March 5, 2018, https://www.nbcnews.com/news/latino/no-permanent-immigration-fix-daca-deadline-dreamers-amp-political-mobilization-n852421 Accessed August 5, 2019.

SELECT BIBLIOGRAPHY

Websites and Articles

Azam, Ahmed, "Migrants' Despair Growing at U.S. Border. So Are Smugglers' Profits," *The New York Times*, January 6, 2019, https://www.nytimes.com/2019/01/06/world/americas/mexico-migrants-smugglers.html Accessed June 3, 2019.

Edelman, Adam, "Sanctuary Cities: Three States, Three Very Different Approaches," NBC News, October 8, 2017, https://www.nbcnews.com/politics/immigration/sanctuary-cities-three-states-three-very-different-approaches-n808406 Accessed June 3, 2019.

Felter, Claire, and Danielle Renwic, "The US Immigration Debate," Council on Foreign Relations, July 2, 2018, https://www.cfr.org/backgrounder/us-immigration-debate-0 Accessed June 3, 2019.

"5 Misconceptions about the U.S.-Mexico border," *Los Angeles Times*, April 5, 2019, https://www.latimes.com/projects/la-na-us-mexico-border-misconceptions/ Accessed June 3, 2019.

"4 Myths about How Immigrants Affect the U.S. Economy," PBS Newshour, November 2, 2018, https://www.pbs.org/newshour/economy/making-sense/4-myths-about-how-immigrants-affect-the-u-s-economy Accessed June 3, 2019.

Gramlich, James, "How Americans See Illegal Immigration, the Border Wall and Political Compromise," Pew Research Center, January 16, 2019, https://www.pewresearch.org/fact-tank/2019/01/16/how-americans-see-illegal-immigration-the-border-wall-and-political-compromise/ Accessed June 3, 2019.

Karas, Tania, "How Does Seeking Asylum Work at the US Border?" PRI's The World, May 1, 2018, https://www.pri.org/stories/2018-05-01/how-does-seeking-asylum-work-us-border Accessed June 3, 2019.

Krogstad, Jens Manuel, and Ana Gonzalez-Barrera, "Key Facts about U.S. Immigration Policies and Proposed Changes," Pew Research Center, May 17, 2019, https://www.pewresearch.org/fact-tank/2019/05/17/key-facts-about-u-s-immigration-policies-and-proposed-changes/ Accessed June 3, 2019.

McMinn, Sean, "Where Does Illegal Immigration Mostly Occur? Here's What The Data Tell Us," NPR, January 10, 2019, https://www.npr.org/2019/01/10/683662691/where-does-illegal-immigration-mostly-occur-heres-what-the-data-tell-us Accessed June 3, 2019.

"Migrant Caravan: What Is It and Why Does It Matter?" BBC News, November 26, 2018, https://www.bbc.com/news/world-latin-america-45951782 Accessed June 3, 2019.

Nunn, Ryan, Jimmy O'Donnell, and Jay Shambaugh, "A Dozen Facts about Immigration," Brookings, October 9, 2018, https://www.brookings.edu/research/a-dozen-facts-about-immigration/ Accessed June 3, 2019.

"Refugees, Asylum-seekers and Migrants," Amnesty International, https://www.amnesty.org/en/what-we-do/refugees-asylum-seekers-and-migrants/ Accessed June 3, 2019.

Rosenblum, Marc R., and Ariel G. Ruiz Soto, "An Analysis of Unauthorized Immigrants in the United States by Country and Region of Birth," Migration Policy Institute, August 2015, https://www.migrationpolicy.org/research/analysis-unauthorized-immigrants-united-states-country-and-region-birth Accessed June 3, 2019.

Ross, Selena, "A Death on the Canadian Border: Dominican Man Was Trying to Reach His Daughter in the U.S.," *The Washington Post*, May 20, 2019, https://www.washingtonpost.com/world/the_americas/a-death-on-the-canadian-border-dominican-man-was-trying-to-reach-his-daughter-in-the-us/2019/05/17/a955bc70-7500-11e9-a7bf-c8a43b84ee31_story.html?utm_term=.bd690802c451 Accessed June 3, 2019.

Rotella, Sebastian, Tim Golden, and ProPublica, "Human Smugglers Are Thriving Under Trump," *The Atlantic*, February 21, 2019, https://www.theatlantic.com/politics/archive/2019/02/human-smugglers-thrive-under-trumps-zero-tolerance/583051/ Accessed June 3, 2019.

Sacchetti, Maria, "You Want a Cookie?': As Families Arrive en Masse, Border Agents Offer Snacks and Medical Checks," *The Washington Post*, February 19, 2019, https://www.washingtonpost.com/local/immigration/you-want-a-cookie-as-families-arrive-en-masse-border-agents-offer-snacks-and-medical-checks/2019/02/19/1b334d5c-1dd7-11e9-9145-3f74070bbdb9_story.html?utm_term=.f06a0bf569af Accessed June 3, 2019.

"U.S. Customs and Border Protection Strategy 2020-2025," U.S. Customs and Border Protection, https://www.cbp.gov/about Accessed June 3, 2019.

"U.S. Immigration Throughout History," USA Facts, June 26, 2018, https://usafacts.org/reports/immigration-history Accessed June 3, 2019.

About the Author

Danielle Smith-Llera taught children to think and write about literature as a teacher before she turned to writing books for them herself. It is a portable career. As the spouse of a U.S. diplomat, she has lived in Washington, D.C., India, Jamaica, and Romania. She is proud to be the descendant of Mexican, Irish, and German immigrants to the United States.

INDEX